Mark T-W-A-I-N!

Mark T-W-A-I-N!

A Story about Samuel Clemens

by David R. Collins
illustrations by Vicky Carey

A Carolrhoda Creative Minds Book

Carolrhoda Books, Inc./Minneapolis

This book is dedicated to Warren Brandt, for his unlimited patience.

This book is available in two editions:
Library binding by Carolrhoda Books, Inc.
Soft cover by First Avenue Editions
c/o The Lerner Group
241 First Avenue North
Minneapolis, MN 55401

Library of Congress Cataloging-in-Publication Data

Collins, David R.
  Mark T-W-A-I-N! : a story about Samuel Clemens / by David R. Collins; illustrated by Vicky Carey.
    p.   cm. — (A Carolrhoda creative minds book)
  Includes bibliographical references (p.   ).
  Summary: Covers the life of the famed nineteenth-century author from his childhood in Hannibal, Missouri, through his careers as journalist, riverboat pilot, soldier, prospector, and humorist.
  ISBN 0-87614-801-1
  1. Twain, Mark, 1835-1910—Biography—Juvenile literature. 2. Authors, American—19th century—Biography—Juvenile literature. [1. Twain, Mark, 1835-1910. 2. Authors, American.] I. Carey, Vicky, ill. II. Title. III. Series.
PS1331.C57   1994
818'.409—dc20
[B]   93-15164
                                                CIP
                                                 AC

Manufactured in the United States of America

2 3 4 5 6 – P/MA – 99 98 97 96 95 94

Table of Contents

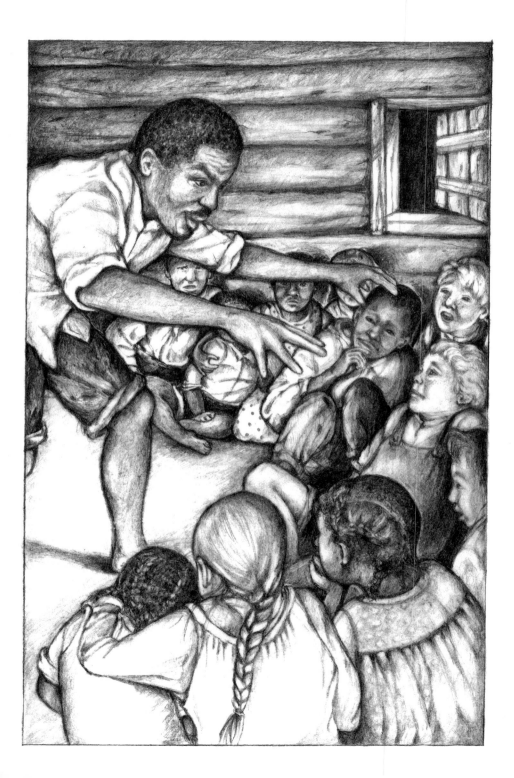

① A Boy's Paradise

No one in Uncle Daniel's one-room log cabin heard the Missouri wind whispering outside. On this August night in the year 1840, all eyes were on Uncle Daniel. Eleven boys and girls huddled on the floor around a crumbling fireplace. A middle-aged black slave shuffled along in front of them, his voice hissing like an angry snake.

Four-year-old Sammy Clemens trembled. He always shook a bit listening to Uncle Daniel's stories. "The Golden Arm" was the best—that dreaded tale of a thief who snatched a ghost's golden arm.

"...and the sad and lonely ghost leaned over the wicked thief's bed and moaned 'W-h-o—g-o-t—m-y—g-o-l-d-e-n—a-r-m?'" The words dripped from Uncle Daniel's lips like thick molasses. Sammy and the others held their breath. They dared not turn away. Uncle Daniel looked for the one most afraid. Then he grabbed the child's shoulders—*"YOU'VE* got it!" he yelled. The cabin burst into screams and nervous giggles. Sammy Clemens never forgot Uncle Daniel's story—Sam told it all his life.

Sammy's life began in another log cabin on November 30, 1835. From August through December that year, people were gazing skyward. Halley's Comet was streaking through the galaxy, as it does every seventy-five years.

The birth of Samuel Clemens in Florida, Missouri, captured far less attention. The baby was the fifth child born to John and Jane Clemens. Though he was named "Samuel" after his grandfather and "Langhorne" in honor of a family friend, he was better known as "Sammy" or "Little Sam."

With a small general store, Sammy's father struggled to support his growing family. Since John Clemens was a lawyer, he offered legal services too. The "judge" as he was called, longed to be rich, and he tried any trade he could. Give him a piece of wood, some pipe, and a few pieces of wire, and he would create a new household gadget. But his gadgets never caught on, and poor harvests kept customers from buying at his store. Late in 1839, when Sammy was four, John loaded up the family and moved thirty miles northeast to Hannibal. There he opened a grocery store.

Hannibal lay tucked between two bluffs along the Mississippi River. Four streets of plain wooden houses and stores stretched one way, eight the other. When the shout of "Steam-boat A-comin!" sounded, the town jolted into activity. That cry summoned everyone to the river. Sammy would wedge his way through the crowd to watch the boat dock.

Like a graceful swan, the riverboat slipped toward the banks. Steam hissed, and a whistle sliced the air. "The sound of that riverboat's whistle raised goosebumps as big as walnuts on me," Sam once wrote. His big dream was to work on a steamboat someday.

As the gangplank was lowered, "roustabouts" unloaded barrels of sugar and molasses from New Orleans, or tools from Pittsburgh, or bolts of silk and satin from the East Coast. Shortly after, they packed up the bales of tobacco and hemp, and the barrels of pork and lard from local farmers.

In only ten minutes, the riverboat was ready to depart. Then Sammy would run off to find his older brother Ben for a swim in Bear Creek or an exploration of the caves and bluffs around Lover's Leap. He thought Hannibal was "a boy's paradise."

Sammy looked just as fondly on his uncle John's farm, which he called "a heavenly place." Sam spent his summers there, near Florida, Missouri. He'd listen to his uncle's jokes and wild tales, and run around with his eight spirited cousins. They made grand playmates, as did the slave children. Together, the youngsters climbed hickory trees, waded in the brook, explored the woods, and begged for Uncle Daniel's scary stories. Yet they all noted a difference between the white and black children. "We were comrades and not comrades," Sammy wrote later. There was an invisible line between the two groups that made it seem that complete friendship was impossible.

Sam once complained to his mother about a black child at the farm who was always singing or whistling. She answered, "Think, he is sold away from his mother; she is in Maryland, a thousand miles from here, and he will never see her again, poor thing. When he is singing, it is a sign that he is not remembering and that comforts me." Though slavery made his mother uncomfortable, it was part of her life. Jennie, a slave girl, did chores around the Clemenses' home.

Whether at home or his uncle's farm, Sammy felt happy, safe, and "out of the Devil's reach."

But Hannibal had its share of murders and strange occurrences, and Jane Clemens worried about her children, especially Sammy. The child nearly drowned in the river three times, and diseases often swept through town. Sam's brother Ben died from one of these illnesses.

Sam, with a shock of sandy red hair topping a pasty-white frame, was puny and weak. He caught colds without half trying. Still, when measles dotted other neighborhood youngsters, Sammy felt left out. To solve the problem, he snuck over to a sick friend's house at night and slid under the covers beside him. Sure enough, he caught the dreaded disease. Red spots covered his body, and a fever raged out of control. Relatives came to say farewell. But Sammy rallied. His mother sighed in relief. "I suppose you were afraid I wouldn't live," remarked Sam.

"No, I was afraid you would," Jane replied, her lips curled in teasing. Though Sam's father was strict and stern, his mother was always telling a joke or an amusing story, often poking fun at herself. "My childhood was filled with warm and wonderful memories," Samuel Clemens later wrote. "None of these happy memories, however, took place inside a schoolhouse."

② The Sting of a Switch

By the late 1830s, every child in Hannibal could receive a formal education for twenty cents a week. Daily lessons covered reading, spelling, good manners, Bible recitations, and arithmetic. Mrs. Elizabeth Horr, a thin, bespectacled, dark-haired woman, ran most classes through the third grade. Each day, she clanged the bell at the entrance of the small log cabin at the end of South Main Street. Sammy was not yet five years old when he started answering that bell.

On his first day, Sammy forgot to stand up when he was asked to recite. Mrs. Horr told him if he broke that rule again, he would get a whipping. Sammy forgot again the same afternoon. He was sent outside to get a suitable switch for his punishment.

Sammy spotted an old, rotted stick. He took it back to the classroom and placed it on the teacher's desk. The teacher looked scornfully down at the boy before her.

"Sam-u-el Lang-horne Cle-mens..."

Never had Sammy heard his full name tied together in one long procession. The sound was frightful. Sammy flinched once more when she ordered another boy to bring back a real switch. That whipping was the first of many. Classroom work bored Sammy, and he broke rules faster than Mrs. Horr could make them.

The arrival of Laura Hawkins, a freckled classmate with pigtails, lifted his spirits. To prove his new love for her, Sam gave her the core of the apple he had eaten at lunch. She thrust the gift back and flounced away.

After Sammy had completed the third grade, Mrs. Horr cheerfully passed him into the hands of

Mr. William Cross. Mr. Cross directed the education of the older boys and girls in another one-room schoolhouse, on the outskirts of Hannibal. When school hours dragged, Sammy would sneak a garter snake into the classroom and let it go. Or he'd daydream about Saturday, when he and his friends would become Robin Hood and his merry men of Sherwood Forest. (Sammy played Robin, of course.) Or he'd make plans to meet Tom Blankenship for some real fun.

Tom Blankenship, who was four years older than Sammy, seemed to lead a life without troubles or worries. Tom's father and mother spent most of their time drinking in the town taverns. The boy slept in a barrel behind the Clemens house and dressed in a "ruin of rags." Tom stayed as far away from school or church as he could. Warned by their parents "to stay away from Tom Blankenship," the boys of Hannibal were even more attracted to him. He taught them how to smoke corncob pipes, how to cuss, and how to hunt for turtle eggs.

Sam took to talking rough, like Tom, and getting into his own share of trouble. Sammy had no use for the Sunday school boys who "sugared up to their folks" for favors.

In the eyes of John and Jane Clemens, Sam's friends Will Bowen and John Briggs were more acceptable companions than Tom. Sammy often convinced them to go swimming or fishing or climbing on the nearby bluffs. Work of any kind was avoided. When it could not be, Sammy turned resourceful.

One day, nine-year-old Sam was caught skipping school. The next Saturday morning, he was sentenced to whitewashing the tall fence around the Clemenses' yard. It was grim work, and Sammy tired of it minutes after starting. When Will and John wandered by, a brilliant thought flashed through his mind. Whistling, Sammy waved the brush grandly across the wooden panels as if he were an artist creating a masterpiece. This was fun, or so one might think.

Sam's friends were intrigued, and before long, he had recruited all kinds of people to do his work. They even paid him to do it. By late afternoon, Sammy's work was done, and he had a collection of doorknobs, apple cores, frogs, and a box of worms—all given to him in exchange for letting his friends swing the whitewash brush.

By the time he was twelve, Sammy was scaling the three hundred feet of Holliday's Hill.

Once, he and Will dislodged a good-sized boulder and rolled it into position on the hill's summit. Patiently, the mischief-makers waited for a wagon to approach. Timing was important. The stone had to be released at just the right moment to scare travelers below without hitting them.

Suddenly, the rock began sliding on its own, and the boys couldn't stop it. A horse pulling a wagon appeared on the road, traveling fast. The two boys shouted and screamed. The driver looked up and saw the boulder rumbling down the hillside, but he couldn't stop the horses in time. At the last minute, the stone flipped into the air and skipped over the entire wagon. Sammy plopped on the ground, his body shaking.

That night, a thunderstorm hit Hannibal. Sammy had heard the minister of the First Presbyterian Church say that lightning often struck people who had sinned. As he shook beneath the covers, Sammy prayed to be spared. He even promised to become a better boy. It was, however, a promise soon forgotten.

"I was fortunate to survive my childhood," Samuel Clemens wrote many years later. "Although there are some folks who might think my survival was *unfortunate*!"

Into Print

While Sam was growing up, the Clemenses moved from house to house, each one smaller and cheaper than the last. Sam had been bringing in wages for the family since he was eleven years old. When he wasn't in school, he was running errands around Hannibal. He made deliveries and did chores for storekeepers, bragging that he "could sweep the cleanest floor west of the Mississippi." Sam hoped his parents might let him quit school if he made enough money.

But they didn't.

Then on March 24, 1847, John Clemens died of pneumonia. Although his father had seldom shown love for his children openly, Sam still took his death hard. The boy kept remembering the times he had misbehaved, all the troubles he had caused. He felt bad that his father had struggled against poverty and died in debt. Sammy feared he would "follow that same path."

Sam's oldest brother, Orion, was now working in St. Louis as a newspaper typesetter, and he sent money home regularly to help his mother. Sam got part-time work at the *Hannibal Gazette*.

In June 1848, his mother let Sam quit school completely, and the twelve year old went to work in the printing shop of Joseph Ament, who published the *Missouri Courier* in Hannibal. Sam was not paid, but he received food, clothes, and a place to sleep, which took these burdens off his family. He slept on a straw mattress on the floor, and his meals were skimpy and watered down. Sam resorted to snitching potatoes and onions from the basement of the shop. For clothes, he wore Ament's hand-me-downs. "His shirts gave me the uncomfortable feeling of living in a circus tent," Sam recalled, "and I had to turn up his pants to my ears to make them short enough."

Despite his misery, Sam had the chance to watch reporters at work. He read their stories as he set them in type and then printed them.

One afternoon, Sam stepped out of the office onto the street. A snappy breeze whipped a piece of paper around his leg. Sam pulled it off and read it slowly. It was a page from a book about Joan of Arc. She sounded so brave and noble.

MISSOURI COURIER

BY JOSEPH AMENT.   Two Dollars a Year.

HANNIBAL, MISSOURI   MONDAY, FEBRUARY 14, 1850.

History in school had never been this interesting! In no time, Sam was reading every history book he could find.

During the summer of 1850, Orion returned home from St. Louis. He bought a printing press and started his own newspaper in Hannibal. The first issue of *The Western Union* appeared in September. The next year, Sam quit his job at the *Courier* and joined Orion and their younger brother, Henry, on the *Union* staff. Sam was given his first chance to write a paragraph or two of news now and then.

Unfortunately, Orion seemed to have inherited his father's bad luck in business. Nothing went right. Advertisers refused to pay their bills. Those who did, paid in produce—a bag of turnips or a bushel of potatoes. Then a fire burned up some of the newspaper machinery. To top everything off, a cow strolled into the office one night and chewed up two of the press's print rollers.

Orion would not give up. In fact, in the fall of 1851, he bought another newspaper—*The Hannibal Journal*—and combined the two papers. He published national news, snippets of "polite literature," and debates over slavery, the expansion of the railroads, and the rights of states to run their own affairs. Sam tried to convince his brother to print more local news and some humor, especially the stories Sam wrote, but Orion would not listen. Subscriptions dropped.

If Orion wouldn't print his stories, Sam thought maybe someone else would. So he sent off his short pieces to publications out East. In May 1852, the *Boston Carpet Bag* printed "The Dandy Fighting the Squatter," by S. L. Clemens, and the *American Courier*, in Philadelphia, printed his historical description of Hannibal. Sam was thrilled.

In September 1852, Orion left for Tennessee. John Clemens had once held land titles there, and Orion wanted to find out if they were worth anything. He put Sam in charge of the *Journal*.

Sam quickly added a little humor and made-up gossip to the *Journal's* pages to create fresh interest in the paper. Breezy tidbits about people in the town written by the reporter W. Epaminandas Adrastas Blab started appearing. "Hannibal Lovers Meet on Dune Site in the Moonlight," one headline declared. Another story poked fun at a rival Hannibal newspaper editor, claiming the gentleman had tried to drown himself in Bear Creek, but found himself "out of his depth" in two inches of water. Sam (alias Mr. Blab) and his imagination ran wild.

So did Orion's temper when he returned. It did not matter that circulation was higher than before. Orion wanted none of Sam's fanciful news. He wanted only the facts.

Sam's humorous tidbits, however, did help the paper. So when Orion returned from another trip in 1853, he promoted Sam and gave him his own column, which Sam gladly filled. But it didn't last. The fortunes of *The Hannibal Journal* continued to slip. The Clemens family moved the newspaper office into their home, and the struggle to survive went on. Finally, Sam decided they would be better off without his mouth to feed.

In June of 1853, seventeen-year-old Sam Clemens boarded a riverboat. He had decided to go to the city of excitement—New York. But he ran out of money by the time he docked in St. Louis, Missouri, where his sister Pamela lived with her husband. So Sam stayed with them and set type at the *St. Louis Evening News* till he earned enough for another ticket. In August, he packed his "duds" and headed east.

Sam arrived in the nation's biggest city with only thirteen dollars to spare. The first thing he did was visit America's first world's fair, held in a huge glass-and-iron building called the Crystal Palace. The average daily attendance at the fair was twice the number of people in Hannibal! Sam wrote home describing all the curiosities he saw, and Orion published Sam's letters in *The Hannibal Journal*. Readers were fascinated by his descriptions and wanted more.

Sam was pleased to comply.

He found a printing job to pay for a room at a cheap boardinghouse. In the evenings, he read for hours in a nearby library. He devoured history books of all kinds, as well as works by William Shakespeare, Charles Dickens, and others. *Don Quixote* by Miguel de Cervantes became an all-time favorite.

The stage also entranced Sam. He loved to go to one of the city's many theaters whenever he had some extra change.

The city, though, made him feel cooped up. People crowded him from all sides. Food was another disappointment. His boardinghouse cook was "villainous." Sam missed Southern cooking—fried chicken, biscuits, and cornbread fresh from the oven. New Yorkers, he moaned, ate only "light bread," stale and stone cold.

A homesick Sam Clemens left New York City in the fall of 1853. His funds carried him only to Philadelphia, where he took a temporary job at the *Philadelphia Inquirer*. In November, Sam learned that his brothers had moved their mother to Muscatine, Iowa, where Orion had bought half interest in another newspaper. A job was waiting for Sam, if he wanted it.

By late summer in 1854, eighteen-year-old Sam was in Iowa. He doubted *The Muscatine Journal* would make it, especially under Orion's direction, but he was glad to be back with his family. He plunged into the newspaper enterprise with full force. Yet he kept on the lookout for new adventures.

In December, Orion married Mary Stotts, of Keokuk, Iowa. He promised her they would move to Keokuk if *The Muscatine Journal* venture did not work out. By March, that fact was clear. Still convinced his place was in printing and publishing, Orion took over the Ben Franklin Book and Job Office in Keokuk. Henry and Sam were invited to come along. Both accepted, though Sam longed to try something new.

A magazine article about folks getting rich on cocoa plantations in South America caught Sam's eye. But he had no funds for the trip.

One morning in October 1856, Sam hurried to work. Something had stuck to his shoe, and he reached down to pull it off. It was a fifty-dollar bill—the most money Sam had ever seen in one spot! That would help pay for a ticket to South America.

Sam's conscience, however, reminded him that he should try to find the owner of the money, so he wrote a newspaper ad. "I didn't describe it particularly," he recalled, "and I waited in daily fear that the owner would turn up and take away my good fortune."

But no one claimed the money. So Sam hurried to the railroad depot and bought a ticket to Cincinnati. From there, he could catch a steamboat south. He also contacted the *Keokuk Post* and agreed to write travel letters for the newspaper for five dollars apiece. He wrote them as if they were from a country bumpkin who was surprised at or misunderstood everything he saw in the big city. Sam signed these humorous letters "Thomas Jefferson Snodgrass."

At Home on the River

It took until April of 1857 for Sam to board "an ancient tub" called the *Paul Jones*. He felt his stomach turn somersaults. Thinking of going to "the mysterious lands" of New Orleans and South America made him "a new being, and the subject of my own admiration."

At every stop, he strolled around the boiler deck and pretended he was a world traveler. While the boat sailed, Sam shadowed the men in the pilot house. He begged Captain Horace Bixby for a chance to hold the wheel and guide the ship. Bixby finally gave in.

As Sam gripped the captain's wheel, visions of his youth rushed back to him. Never had Sam felt such power and control. In his mind, the Mississippi River pilot was the freest and most independent person on earth. What more could any man ask? Sam's thoughts of South America faded swiftly.

By the time the boat docked in New Orleans, Sam was pleading with Captain Bixby to train him as a riverboat pilot. "Cub pilots are more trouble than they're worth!" the crusty old captain declared. But Sam wore him down. He persuaded Bixby to teach him to pilot between New Orleans and St. Louis.

Sam thought that "all a pilot had to do was to keep his boat in the water." That notion changed fast. Bixby insisted his pupil know every snag, sandbar, point, and island in the Mississippi, in daytime and night. On the way back to St. Louis, the captain moved away from the wheel. "Here," Bixby said, "take her; and shave those steamboats as close as you'd peel an apple."

Sam did his best to learn, and he always carried a notebook, as the captain requested, jotting down everything he heard and saw on the water. The language of the river workers had its own code. As the leadsman on the boat pulled his measuring device (a piece of lead on twine) out of the river, he'd call out, "mark three!" which meant three fathoms, or eighteen feet, deep.

Minutes later, another shout would ring out, "mark T-W-A-I-N!" The boat had slipped into water two fathoms, or twelve feet, deep. Mark twain was the safety point, but just barely, for any decent-sized vessel. "Mark one" meant trouble—one fathom of water was too shallow for travel.

In April 1859, Sam got his piloting license. He began working as a cub pilot on various river-boats. He got his brother Henry a job with him on *The Pennsylvania* as a "mud-clerk," count-ing coal boxes and measuring woodpiles. One night, while Sam was steering, trouble broke out. The chief pilot accused Henry of lying and hit him in the face. Sam "left the boat to steer itself, and avenged the insult." He banged a chair over the man's head. The captain ordered Sam off the ship at New Orleans for one trip—though Henry was allowed to stay on board.

On *The Pennsylvania's* next journey, four of the ship's boilers exploded. Henry Clemens was blown into the water. Hearing the screams and shouts of others on board, he swam back to help. More explosions shook the boat.

Henry was badly crushed and scalded. Sam had been following *The Pennsylvania* in another steamboat. When he docked at Memphis, he found out that his brother was dying. He sat by his bedside for six days, until Henry died. Sam felt responsible for his death since he had gotten him the job. He promised himself to become the safest riverboat pilot possible.

Sam Clemens *was* a fine pilot, memorizing every foot of the rivers he traveled. He became a favorite among other pilots for telling amazing stories about near-disasters. No one seemed to mind when Sam "stretched the truth."

Whether telling tales on a riverboat's upper deck or seated at a dining table enjoying cigars and brandy, Sam became more and more aware of an uneasiness sweeping the nation. Politicians argued constantly and fervently about slavery and the right of the government in Washington, D.C., to tell states what to do. Then Southern states started pulling out of the Union, which President Lincoln would not allow. In 1861, the sounds of guns thundered. The country was at war.

Because of battles over the Mississippi, steamboats no longer traveled the whole length of the river. Sam was soon out of a job, and he didn't want to be a warship pilot, so he returned to Hannibal. He flip-flopped between declaring himself in favor of the Union and of the

Confederacy. His brother Orion supported Lincoln and felt slaves should be freed. Sam agreed. "We might look different on the outside," he wrote later, "but under the skin are the same parts."

But Sam eventually decided to become a Confederate soldier, mostly out of loyalty to some childhood pals in Hannibal. With fourteen others, Sam "set off to soldier." The new Marion Rangers (named for their county) swore to be faithful to the State of Missouri and to drive all invaders from her soil. Then the Rangers set off to find an organized unit of the Confederate Army. But when they came upon a perfect spot for fishing and swimming, the men did that instead.

Patriotic spirit among the Marion Rangers disappeared within two weeks. There was no wish to drill and march, and there was not enough ammunition to practice shooting. It rained and rained. When word reached the men that Union soldiers were looking for them, the Marion Rangers hightailed it back to Hannibal and disbanded. "It was our finest decision," observed Sam Clemens.

5

The Wild, Wild West

'Giddyap, you varmints!"

At the stage driver's orders, Sam smiled and leaned back in his seat. He was glad to look to a more promising future.

Although the State of Missouri had forgiven Sam for his short-lived career as a soldier, he still had feared the Union army might force him to pilot one of their warships. He hadn't known what to do. But, as usual, Orion had had a proposition for him. When he lived in St. Louis, Orion had worked for a lawyer named Edward Bates. After Abraham Lincoln became president, he named Bates the nation's attorney general. Bates, in turn, named Orion Clemens the secretary of the Territory of Nevada. Now Orion wanted his own secretary—his brother Sam. Eager to get out of Missouri till the war ended, Sam had agreed.

In July of 1861, the stagecoach carrying the Clemens brothers rolled west across the prairies, deserts, and mountains, as they made their way to the rough, unsettled western territories. Sam witnessed buffalo hunts, coyotes, sagebrush, pony express riders, and the "unspeakably picturesque" westerners—with their ten-gallon hats, boots, tight pants, bowie knives, and pistols.

Finally, after twenty days, the Clemenses arrived in Nevada's capital, Carson City. It was a scattered collection of wooden buildings and canvas tents, with the snowcapped Sierra Nevadas behind them. Sam and Orion got off the dusty stage, grabbed their bags, and took a room at Mrs. Murphy's boardinghouse. Orion took the downstairs room, and Sam settled himself upstairs, joining a group of thirteen other men, each hired to work for the new governor, James Nye.

But the "Brigade," as they called themselves, soon found there was nothing to do, other than a little surveying now and then. Each day, they wandered over to the tavern to play cards and pass the time. They also collected tarantulas and scorpions in glass jars on the wall shelf.

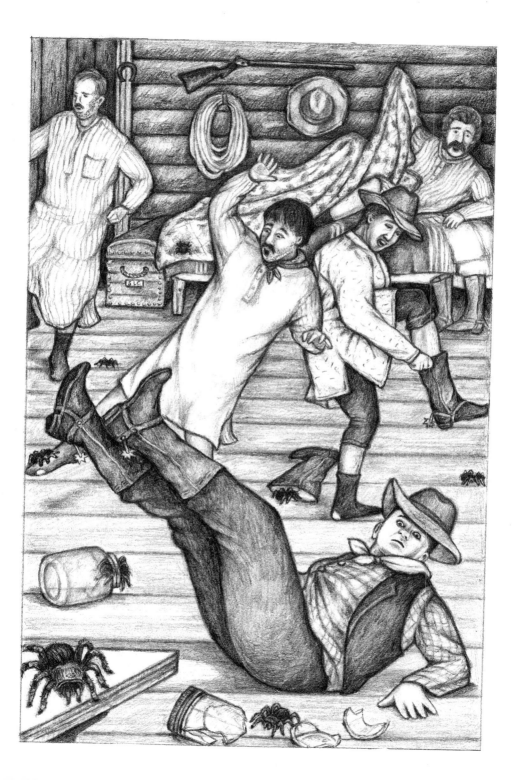

One night, young Bob Howland, a member of the Brigade, came home late from the tavern. He accidentally stumbled against the wall, knocking the jars off the shelf and sending their occupants scurrying in all directions. "Turn out, boys!" Howland shouted. "The tarantulas is loose!" Nightshirted men leaped out of beds, colliding with one another, as they scampered to flee the small attackers. Sam got a good story out of that!

With his new "job," Sam had plenty of time for storytelling—and anything else he wanted to do. One day, with a buddy, John Kinney, Sam set out for a visit to Lake Tahoe. It was a grueling hike across flatlands, hills, and valleys. But suddenly, the magnificent lake "burst" upon the weary walkers. The clear blue water, tinged here and there with green, was a perfect mirror for the peaks of the mountains surrounding it. "Whenever I think of it I want to go there and die, the place is so beautiful," Sam wrote to his sister Pamela. He and Kinney planned to stake a claim on the timber around the lake.

Then disaster struck. Preparing for supper, Sam lit a campfire. Dry pine needles on the ground sparked and roared into a blazing carpet. Within moments, nearby thickets of manzanita, huckleberry, oak, and pine were wrapped in flames. The two campers were lucky to escape alive. Sam's thoughts of a fortune from a timber claim had gone up in smoke.

Sam tried prospecting for silver next. He joined an engineer named Calvin Higbie in the mountains. They lived in a ten-by-twelve-foot "mansion" with a dirt floor and canvas roof. Sam didn't mind the rough life. Sporting his red mustache and beard, a battered slouch hat, and the same flannel shirt each day, he felt good and "rowdyish."

When Calvin Higbie discovered traces of a rich silver deposit, Sam began planning what to do with his riches. All they needed to do was to file a claim and work it before the ten-day deadline. But then Calvin was summoned to California to give advice about some cement mines. No matter. He left a note for Sam so he could work the mine. But the same night, Sam was called away to help Orion care for the governor's sick brother. He too left a letter, without noticing his friend's note.

Both men dreamed of the mounds of silver they would have when they returned. Ten days later, they ran into each other at the cabin and found other men mining there. The claim deadline had come and gone—and so had their chances to be rich. Years later, Sam dedicated a book to Calvin H. Higbie, "an honest man, a genial comrade, and a steadfast friend . . . in memory of the curious time when we two were millionaires for ten days."

Since he couldn't strike it rich with timber or silver, Sam sent some of his stories to *The Territorial Enterprise* in Virginia City, Nevada. Not only did the newspaper print Sam's work, but the editor offered him a full-time job as city editor at twenty-five dollars a week. "I snatched up the offer like a bandit!" Sam recalled.

The Territorial Enterprise gave its readers a lot of variety. Gunslingers roamed Virginia City, ready to shoot crooked gamblers or anyone else who got in their way. Announcements were made of church socials, school picnics, and the arrival of newcomers. When news was scarce, Sam turned on his own creative juices. He poked fun at local politicians and told stories about ghosts roaming the city. Sometimes he signed his work "Josh," just for fun, but most often he used the name "Mark Twain," in honor of his golden days of steamboat piloting.

Sam was beginning to feel that his humor and news reports could be used for "crusading journalism"—for pointing out problems in society. He wrote to another editor, "It is your duty to ferret out abuses and seek to correct them." Sam learned much about grammar, accuracy, and humor from the other men on the newspaper. William Wright, who used the pen name Dan DeQuille, was also a humorist. He and Sam became close friends, reading each other's stories and sharing pranks.

In December 1863, Artemus Ward came to Virginia City. His real name was Charles Farrar Browne, and he traveled from town to town giving humorous talks. Sam covered Ward's visit for the newspaper, and he, Dan, and Artemus became a rowdy threesome. The young writers roared at Ward's exaggerated tales and imitations of eccentric characters.

When Sam showed Artemus some of his printed stories, the actor smiled. "I put on stage what you put on paper," he said. Ward asked Sam to "leave sage-brush obscurity" and come to New York to write and give talks. Politely, Sam declined. He didn't feel ready to burst out on the audiences in the East. But he agreed to send a story for Artemus's upcoming book.

In the meantime, Sam was given a raise to forty

dollars a week, and newspapers in California began reprinting some of his stories. Mark Twain became one of the most well-known writers in Nevada, and he was recognized throughout the West. Readers looked forward to his outlandish descriptions and wisecracking humor. They were also ready for him to poke fun at somebody—especially lazy or dishonest government workers—to bring their failings out into the open.

Of course, the people at the butt ends of Sam's jokes often missed the humor. Once Sam made up a story about a murder that was so gruesome that even the westerners of Carson City and California were disgusted. He apologized in print, but not long afterward, he criticized a city leader, who got so angry he challenged Sam to a duel. Being better with words than a gun, Sam talked the man out of it.

The final straw came when Sam wrote a funny story accusing some women in the community of stealing the funds raised at a charity ball. It was printed by accident, but it so outraged the whole community that Sam was too embarassed to stay in Virginia City.

So by the spring of 1864, Sam was looking around for new adventures. With the Civil War still going on, there was no hope for piloting on the Mississippi. Sam set his compass for the West Coast and San Francisco.

Soon after his arrival, Sam began writing news reports for a paper called the *Morning Call*. It was dull work. He managed to write some cutting articles on the crookedness and brutality of the city's police force, but there was little chance to display his style and imagination. So he quit and started writing stories to send to two literary magazines, the *Golden Era* and the *Californian*.

At the *Californian*, he met two important editors, Charles Henry Webb and Bret Harte. These two men helped Sam fine-tune his "country bumpkin" style of humor into a witty, sophisticated style. They "trimmed and trained and schooled me," said Sam.

Yet times were hard for Sam, and he was barely making enough to live on. He felt depressed and lonely. When two friends, Jim Gillis and Dick Stoker, suggested prospecting in the Tuolumne Hills outside of the city, Sam packed his bags. They camped near Jackass Hill and panned for gold.

At night, they sat around the campfire and swapped stories. Jim was a master storyteller.

He told of a cat that was an expert gold miner and a blue jay that could talk. At a nearby mining camp, the tall tales and yarns were thickly spun too. Sam heard Ben Coon, an old-timer there, tell his story: "There was once a fellow who owned a frog," he began in a solemn voice. "Now this here frog was a real jumper, able to leap over any rock or bush..." Sam relished each detail. If he could find no gold, he could at least enjoy the search.

Before long, the supplies and money ran out, and Sam returned to San Francisco. He still had no steady job. The war was over now, and Sam considered returning to piloting riverboats. But he didn't want to return to the eastern states a failure, and writing had grabbed ahold of him. He took a job working as the San Francisco reporter for his old employer—*The Territorial Enterprise*—and sent other pieces to the *Californian* and the *Dramatic Chronicle*. Some of his pieces were reprinted in journals on the East Coast.

Encouraged by these successes, Sam sat down to write the story he had promised to Artemus Ward for his book. He tried to capture the character and western voice of the solemn old miner,

Ben Coon. Though Artemus's book was already done, he liked Sam's story so much he sent it on to a New York paper. "Jim Smiley and the Jumping Frog" appeared in New York's *Saturday Press* on November 18, 1865. The story "set all New York in a roar," said a reviewer.

Early the next year, Sam persuaded the editors of the *Sacramento Union* to send him to the Sandwich Islands (now known as Hawaii) to write a special series about the plantations there. While he was on the islands, an open boat carrying fifteen men in a "helpless and starving condition" drifted ashore. Their clipper ship had burned, and they had been adrift for forty-three days. Sam interviewed the men, sending his report speedily back to the *Union* offices. The grim, graphic details of the survivors' ordeals appeared first in the *Union* and were then picked up by other papers. Mark Twain had caused a stir again.

Upon his return, a friend encouraged Sam to take his stories of the Sandwich Islands to the stage, as Artemus Ward did. Maybe the stage was worth a try, Sam thought. He had done other foolish things in his life. One more wouldn't matter much.

⑥

Want to Hear a Story?

DOORS OPEN AT 7 O'CLOCK
THE TROUBLE WILL START AT 8

The posters announced Mark Twain's first public show. Sam was sure no one would pay a dollar to hear him. He couldn't eat all day.

That evening, October 2, 1866, people packed into the Academy of Music in San Francisco. The full house gave Sam courage. Thirty-year-old Sam moved around the stage, swinging his watch chain or twiddling his black cigar. His reddish-brown mustache wiggled as he spoke. He told his tales in his slow Southern drawl, pausing at just the right moments, acting as if nothing was the least bit funny. His audience felt as if they were old friends, and their laughter bounced off the walls like thunder.

Happy with his reception, Sam took his story-telling on the road, to other western cities and towns. One newspaper reviewer in Nevada City wrote, "We think that 'Mark Twain' as a lecturer is far superior to 'Artemus Ward' or any of that class." It was the highest of compliments.

While on the road, Sam found a publisher for a group of short stories. In May 1867, Charles Henry Webb, his editor friend, published Mark Twain's first book: *The Celebrated Frog of Calaveras County and Other Sketches*.

After his book was out and selling well, Sam convinced the *Alta California* newspaper to finance a five-month trip to Europe and North Africa in exchange for stories of what he saw. Sam wrote letters back about France, Italy, Greece, Egypt, and the Holy Land, as well as about the other travelers. Sam changed their names, "for the individual's protection and more importantly, my own."

While Sam was visiting with a fellow traveler on the ship, Charles Langdon, he noticed a portrait of a youthful woman painted on ivory. Soft dark curls framed a delicate white face and a pleas-ant smile. Charles promised Sam to introduce his sister once they returned to the United States.

The opportunity arrived in December of 1867. After a few meetings with Charles's family, Sam accompanied Charles and his sister, Olivia, to a public reading by the British author Charles Dickens in New York City. All through the performance, Sam stole glances at Olivia.

Sam's busy lecturing and writing schedule, though, left him little free time to see Olivia, who lived in Elmira, New York. So he had to woo her by mail. A quiet and shy girl, Olivia was overwhelmed by the cigar-puffing, tough-talking fellow from the West. She nicknamed him "Youth," while he called her "Livy." When he proposed, she declined. She didn't like his swearing, drinking, and gambling. He promised to change.

While Sam worked on convincing Olivia to marry him, her father, Jervis Langdon, worked against the match. He was a wealthy, respected man, and he failed to see Sam as a suitable mate for his daughter. Sam's family seemed undistinguished, his background suspicious, and his future as a journalist questionable. True, Sam had had one book published, and his travel letters were going to be collected in another, but that didn't mean Sam could support a family.

Six weeks after her refusal, Olivia gave in. But it took her father until February 1869. A year later, Olivia Langdon married Samuel Clemens. He was thirty-five; she was twenty-six. As a wedding gift, Jervis gave the newlyweds a three-story brick mansion in Buffalo, New York, complete with a cook, housemaid, and butler-coachman. Jervis also loaned Sam money to buy part ownership in the *Buffalo Express*. Sam had clearly won him over.

After spending a honeymoon year in Buffalo, Sam and Livy sold the newspaper and moved to Hartford, Connecticut. Sam wanted to live near his publisher, the American Publishing Company in Hartford, as he worked on his new book.

Sam's travel letters, which had been published by the American Publishing Company in *Innocents Abroad,* had attracted thousands of readers to Mark Twain. They liked how he mocked the stuffy, old-fashioned culture of Europe. Even so, American literary critics had considered Twain's work "lightweight" and "cute." Sam wanted the respect of other authors. "Just write what you know," his family and friends told him. So Sam started writing his real and made-up Old West adventures for a volume called *Roughing It*.

By the end of 1872, *Innocents Abroad* had sold over 100,000 copies, *Roughing It* was selling well too, and as a lecturer, Mark Twain was bringing in five hundred dollars a night.

Sam's achievements helped soften the sadnesses that shadowed the early years of his marriage. The death of his father-in-law, Jervis Langdon, was a bitter blow. Then Livy's friend Emma Nye fell victim to typhoid fever. Emma's sudden death upset Livy so much that her first child, Langdon Clemens, was born early. Never healthy, the infant died a year and half later.

Sam tried to escape his personal grief by writing. Disgusted with the meaningless novels being published, he joined talents with his Hartford neighbor Charles Dudley Warner to do something better. Their book, *The Gilded Age*, exposed some of the crime and corruption in the government after the Civil War. People scrambled to buy copies.

Enjoying his newfound wealth, Sam built a grand mansion in Hartford. Giant rooms, porches, balconies, turrets, a plant-filled conservatory, a billiard room, and countless cats—all were included. There was plenty of space to write, to play host to other authors, and to throw tantrums. Sam was known for his hot temper—as well as for his old habits of cussing, drinking, and gambling, which had returned.

On his free time, Sam played around with inventions. "I never saw a machine or gadget that couldn't be improved," he wrote. Always looking for quick money, Sam invested in other people's inventions too. None made him rich.

Meanwhile, the Clemens family grew. First came Susan Olivia, then Clara, and finally, a third daughter, Jean. Sam smothered "his girls" with love and presents. "You're spoiling them all, Youth!" Livy would complain.

By the mid 1870s, the issue of slavery and his role in it as a white southerner had started to gnaw at Sam. He wrote a tale in which an old ex-slave tells her harsh life story. He based her experiences on those of Aunty Cord, the cook at Livy's sister's farm, whom Sam greatly respected.

"A True Story" was printed in *Atlantic* magazine in November 1874. William Dean Howells, a famous editor and critic, wrote, "the rugged truth of the sketch leaves all other stories of slave life far behind and reveals a gift in the author for the simple, dramatic report of reality which we have seen equaled in no other American writer."

Sam followed up on the story by lecturing at African American churches and working for improved rights for blacks. He also paid in part for an African American artist's schooling in Paris and a law student's courses at Yale.

Having looked back at his childhood, Sam decided to write another book about it. He gave Hannibal the new name of St. Petersburg. Then he invented Tom Sawyer, who had a little of Sam's personality, while Huck Finn seemed much like Tom Blankenship, Becky Thatcher like Laura Hawkins, and Aunt Polly like an older version of his mother. Whitewashing the fence, skipping school, and river rafting were there too. In 1876, *The Adventures of Tom Sawyer* appeared, to the delight of Twain's fans.

Sam did most of his writing in Hartford or at Quarry Farm near Elmira, New York, where Livy's sister Susan lived. Livy helped Sam's writing career by reading his manuscripts and offering comments. "She could have opened a school for editors," Sam wrote later. "Always she sensed just the right word and the right thought that should be written. I thought about renting her out to other writers but she would have none of it."

When Sam tired of his writing routine or needed

money, he went lecturing around the country. He packed up the family in 1879 and took them overseas to England. The British treated Sam like a king. Despite the royal treatment, Sam "was glad to get home." He shared the best and the worst of the travels with his readers in *A Tramp Abroad*. The trip also inspired the tale *The Prince and the Pauper* about life in England without money.

During the next twenty years, Sam Clemens juggled a busy schedule of writing and public speaking. The plays he wrote did poorly, but each new book and lecture brought him praise. About *Life on the Mississippi*, which appeared in book form in 1883, one reviewer wrote: "You will love every drop of this magnificent river after reading Twain's book."

Two years later, the author brought back some favorite characters in *The Adventures of Huckleberry Finn*. This time, he let Huck tell his story in his own carefree language: "You don't know me without you have read a book by the name of *The Adventures of Tom Sawyer*; but that ain't no matter." Critics hailed the book as truly American writing. Many white southerners disliked the book, though, because it made them look cruel and petty. And in the book, Huck changes from looking at the slave Jim as a piece of property to seeing him as a friend. (Jim is based on Uncle Daniel.) Jim might be superstitious, but Huck sees he has more dignity and a better heart than the rest of the people Huck meets.

During the early 1880s, Sam and his nephew Charles L. Webster had started a publishing house. The profits from *Huck Finn* helped the partners finance the publishing of the autobiography of General Ulysses S. Grant, the former president. Grant was writing his life story to free his family from debts. The general finished the manuscript four days before he died. Sam edited it himself. When it was published, it became a best seller. Proudly, Sam gave Mrs. Grant a check for $200,000—seventy percent of the profits. In all, Grant's family received about half a million dollars from the memoirs.

Returning to his own writing, Sam published *A Connecticut Yankee in King Arthur's Court* in 1889. The humorous story of a man from the United States tossed back in time to England's age of knighthood became an instant success.

Although writing brought in hefty sums, Sam's outside investments drained him. He poured money into a sound machine (Alexander Graham

Bell beat him to it), an ink pen (it leaked), and a typesetter (the keys stuck). Even his publishing house failed, leaving stacks of bills. It took years to pay them.

Sam thought his family could live cheaper in Europe so he moved with them there. He filled theaters wherever he lectured, and audiences proclaimed Mark Twain "America's Greatest Humorist."

Though lecturing often, Sam had not put down his pen. He believed writing was an art. "The difference between the right word and the almost right word is the difference between lightning and the lightning bug," he declared.

In 1895, Sam's daughter Susan became ill and died of meningitis. Sam and the family moved back to the United States. In spite of his deep grief, he completed more stories about Tom Sawyer and *Personal Recollections of Joan of Arc*—a history of the French heroine he first encountered on the flyaway page so long ago.

A new century loomed ahead. Sam had become so famous and respected for his humorous wisdom that a common joke was "Who's president of the United States?" The answer would be, "Well, if it's not Mark Twain, I don't know. And if he isn't president, he should be."

(7) The Comet Returns

As the 20th century dawned, Mark Twain was quoted across the country—and beyond. His clever comments were memorable because of the bite of truth in them. Sam cut down crooked politicians with a particularly sharp sword. "There's only one spot windier than the eye of a tornado," he would say. "That's the mouth of a politician."

In 1902, Sam was invited back to Hannibal to hand out diplomas to the graduating seniors of the high school. As always, he dressed for the occasion in his all-white suit. He was sixty-six, with bushy white hair and blue-gray eyes that still sparkled. His step had slowed some though. He told the crowd, "My own bottom still tingles from the switchings I received from my teachers. Now I'm handing out diplomas. Life takes some strange turns indeed."

Those turns darkened when his beloved Livy began to suffer heart problems. Hoping a climate change might help, Sam took her to Italy. The effort failed, and on June 4, 1904, Olivia Langdon Clemens died. Sam brought her back to be buried in Elmira beside their daughter Susan.

As always, Sam turned to his writing to release his emotions. His articles and stories grew bitter. In the past, he had used humor to point out people's and governments' failings so they could change for the better. Now he felt less hopeful about people and the world. "If we shot every foolish politician in this country, it would be a much quieter world," he observed. "It is a thought worth pondering." Much of the humor was gone in Mark Twain, but his powerful words still dug deeply into the human heart.

In 1907, Sam again traveled to England, where he received a Doctor of Literature degree from Oxford University. As he paraded about in long red robes, it made him smile to hear himself hailed as "a scholar of the world."

Sam wanted to write one more book before he died—his own life story. At first, he planned to have it published after his death. But when a magazine, the *North American Review*, offered him thirty thousand dollars just for the beginning of the book, Sam changed his mind. He wrote the first chapters and used the money he received to build a new summer house in Redding, Connecticut. He wanted a place his daughters could share, with plenty of cats, of course, and a deluxe billiard room. "I'm not a fussy man," he insisted. The rest of the time, he planned to live in Bermuda.

In November 1909, Clara Clemens married a Russian pianist, Ossip Gabrilowitsch, and moved out of the family home in Redding. The following month, Jean Clemens suffered a heart attack and died, leaving Sam all alone.

Halley's Comet was due back in the year 1910, for its first visit in seventy-six years. Sam Clemens had entered the world during its last visit, in 1835, and he often predicted, "I came with the comet, I will leave with it."

Sure enough, Sam Clemens did as he promised. On April 21, 1910, he died, as Halley's Comet blazed across the galaxy.

"America wears no smiles today," wrote one newspaper editor. "The man who made us laugh at ourselves is gone."

Books by Mark Twain
(Samuel Langhorne Clemens) include:

1867 *The Celebrated Jumping Frog of Calaveras County and Other Sketches*

1869 *The Innocents Abroad*

1872 *Roughing It*

1873 *The Gilded Age* (with C. D. Warner)

1876 *The Adventures of Tom Sawyer*

1880 *A Tramp Abroad*

1882 *The Prince and the Pauper; The Stolen White Elephant*

1883 *Life on the Mississippi*

1885 *The Adventures of Huckleberry Finn*

1889 *A Connecticut Yankee in King Arthur's Court*

1892 *The American Claimant*

1893 *The £100,000 Bank Note*

1894 *Tom Sawyer Abroad; The Tragedy of Pudd'nhead Wilson and the Comedy of Those Extraordinary Twins*

1896 *Personal Recollections of Joan of Arc; Tom Sawyer Abroad, Tom Sawyer Detective, and Other Stories*

1897 *How to Tell a Story and Other Essays; Following the Equator*

1900 *The Man that Corrupted Haddleyburg and Other Stories*

1916 *The Mysterious Stranger*

1938 *Letters from the Earth*

Bibliography

Clemens, Clara. *My Father, Mark Twain.* New York: Harper & Brothers, 1931.

Clemens, Samuel L. *Mark Twain's Autobiography.* A. B. Paine, ed., New York: Harper, 1924.

Clemens, Samuel L. *The Autobiography of Mark Twain.* Charles Neider, ed., New York: Harper & Row, 1959.

Clemens, Samuel L. *Mark Twain Speaking.* Paul Fatout, ed., Iowa City: University of Iowa Press, 1976.

Gerber, John C. *Mark Twain.* Boston: G. K. Hall & Co., 1988.

Hoff, Rhoda. *Why They Wrote.* New York: Henry Z. Walck, Inc., 1961.

Kaplan, Justin. *Mark Twain & His World.* New York: Simon & Schuster, 1974.

Lauber, John. *The Making of Mark Twain: A Biography.* New York: American Heritage, 1985.

Sanborn, Margaret. *Mark Twain—The Bachelor Years.* New York: Doubleday, 1990.

Unger, Leonard, ed., *American Writers—A Collection of Literary Biographies, Volume 4.* New York: Charles Scribner's Sons, 1974.